# Usborne Beginners
# Eggs and chicks

### Fiona Patchett
### Designed by Josephine Thompson
### and Nicola Butler

Illustrated by Tetsuo Kushii and Zoe Wray

Bird consultant: Dr. S. James Reynolds

Reading consultant: Alison Kelly

# Contents

# Parents and chicks

All birds lay eggs which hatch into chicks. Most birds take care of their chicks as they grow.

Penguin chicks stay close together to keep warm. Their parents stand nearby.

# Building a nest

Most birds build nests to keep their eggs safe. They use things they find nearby to build them.

This puffin collects grass to fill its nest.

A bird brings twigs to a tree. It uses its beak to join them together.

It adds moss, roots and grass, and makes them into a cup shape.

The bird presses down to make a hollow in the nest.

Chaffinches can make 1,300 trips a day to collect things for their nests.

# Unusual nests

Nests can be many shapes and sizes. Some birds have very clever ways of building nests.

A tailorbird makes a row of holes around a leaf.

It sews the leaf shut with cobwebs, then fills it with feathers.

A hummingbird's nest is tiny. It is made from cobwebs and plants.

Weaverbirds build grass
nests that hang from branches.

Cave swiftlets make
their nests from spit.

# Laying eggs

Some birds don't lay their eggs in a nest. They lay them in different places.

Guillemots lay eggs on cliffs. Their eggs are pointed.

If an egg is pushed, it rolls in a circle. It does not roll off the cliff.

Black skimmers lay their eggs on sandy beaches.

Flamingos lay their eggs
on mounds of mud.

Kingfishers lay their
eggs in holes on riverbanks.

# Keeping warm

Birds need to keep their eggs warm so a chick can grow inside.

An emperor penguin balances its egg on its feet. Its body keeps the egg warm.

Penguins balance their egg on their feet for two months.

Mallee fowls bury their eggs under soil and leaves. The leaves rot and give out heat, which keeps the eggs warm.

A bird may lose feathers on its chest.

The bare area helps keep its eggs warm.

# Inside an egg

When an egg is laid, a chick starts to grow inside.

The red spot on the yolk starts to grow into a chick.

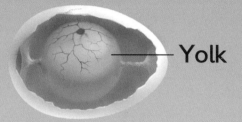 Yolk

The yolk contains food which helps the chick to grow.

Chick

The chick grows bigger. The white protects the chick.

White

8

Chicks take from 10 days to 75 days to grow inside an egg.

The chick grows to look like a tiny bird with a beak, eyes and feet.

A chick cheeps inside its egg. Its parents can hear its call.

# Hatching

When a chick is strong enough, it hatches from its egg.

Egg tooth

1. A chick has a lump on its beak called an egg tooth.

2. It uses its egg tooth to make holes around the shell.

3. The chick pushes the top off the egg, then rests for a while.

4. The chick struggles out of the shell. Its feathers are damp.

The chick's feathers dry
and become fluffy.

The chick doesn't need its
egg tooth. Soon it drops off.

# In the nest

Chicks born in nests have thin feathers. They stay in the nest until more feathers grow.

1. Chicks are born with closed eyes.

2. Feathers start to grow on their bodies.

3. After a few days, their eyes open.

4. Soon the chicks don't fit in the nest.

These egret chicks
have to grow
stronger feathers
before they can
leave the nest.

# Cuckoo chicks

Some cuckoos don't build nests. They lay their eggs in the nests of other birds.

A cuckoo lays its egg in another bird's nest and flies away.

The bird sits on the nest and keeps all the eggs warm.

When the cuckoo hatches, it pushes out the other eggs.

Cuckoo chicks call again and again so adult birds will bring them more food.

A cuckoo chick is often bigger than the adult bird which feeds it.

# Dinnertime

Chicks need lots of food to help them grow. They eat things like insects, seeds or fish.

Fairy terns feed their chicks with fish. The chick swallows the fish whole.

Some chicks try to push other chicks away to get the most food.

A mother arrives with a worm. Her chicks open their mouths.

She pushes the worm into a chick's mouth and flies off for more.

A chick's mouth is very bright inside. This shows its parents where to put food.

# First flight

Chicks know how to fly when they hatch, but they need to be strong before they leave the nest.

Chicks try flapping their wings a lot.

When their wings are strong, they jump from the nest.

They stretch their wings and glide to the ground.

Some birds ignore their chicks
so they have to leave their nest
to look for food.

This baby fairy tern
is flapping its wings,
but it can't fly until its
feathers have grown.

# Good parents

Birds take care of their chicks until they are big enough to take care of themselves.

Swans carry their chicks on their backs. Baby swans are called cygnets.

Male swans scare animals away from their cygnets by puffing up their feathers.

Some chicks hide in their mother's feathers to keep safe.

In hot places, birds have to keep their chicks cool.

An emu uses its body to protect its chicks from the sun.

A shoebill showers its chick with water to keep it cool.

# Growing up

Baby birds learn how to take care of themselves by watching their parents.

These houbara bustard chicks are learning how to hunt for food by watching their mother.

Chicks copy the songs their parents sing.

Chicks follow the first thing they see. It is usually their mother.

If they see another animal, they think that animal is their mother.

Ducklings know how to swim as soon as they hatch. They don't need to learn.

# Different eggs

Some eggs are plain and some are speckled. There are lots of shapes and sizes of eggs.

Plovers lay their eggs among stones on beaches.

The eggs are speckled. They are hard to spot among the stones.

When the chicks hatch, they are hard to spot too.

Arctic
tern egg

Kestrel
egg

Blue-winged
pitta egg

American
robin egg

All these eggs are their actual size. This ostrich egg is the biggest kind of egg.

Hummingbird eggs are the smallest.

American golden plover egg

# Glossary of bird words

Here are some of the words in this book you might not know. This page tells you what they mean.

 nest - a place that birds build to keep their eggs and chicks safe.

 yolk - the yellow part in the middle of an egg. It helps the chick to grow.

 hatch - when a chick breaks out of its egg through the shell.

 egg tooth - the part of a chick's beak which it uses to break the egg shell.

 cygnet - a baby swan.

 duckling - a baby duck.

 speckled - covered with little dots that make a pattern.

# Web sites to visit

If you have a computer, you can find out more about eggs and chicks on the Internet. On the Usborne Quicklinks Web site there are links to four fun Web sites.

Web site 1 - Watch a movie about birds.

Web site 2 - Find out more about birds and make a pop-up bird card.

Web site 3 - Look at pictures of eggs and chicks in a nest.

Web site 4 - Watch a video of chicks feeding.

To visit these Web sites, go to **www.usborne-quicklinks.com** and type the keywords "beginners eggs and chicks". Then, click on the link for the Web site you want to visit. Before you use the Internet, look at the safety guidelines inside the back cover of this book and ask an adult to read them with you.

# Index

## Acknowledgements

Managing editor: Fiona Watt, Managing designer: Mary Cartwright

**Photo credits**

The publishers are grateful to the following for permission to reproduce material.
**Cover** GettyImages/Tim Flach and Andy Sacks  **p1** GettyImages/Laurie Campbell. **p2-3** Windrush Photos/David Tipling. **p4** Kevin Shafer/CORBIS. **p6** Michael and Patricia Fogden/CORBIS. **p7** Warren Photographic/Kim Taylor. **p8** Dan Guravich/CORBIS. **p9** Nature Stock Shots/Mary Helsaple. **p10** Robert Schoen/Still Pictures. **p11** Bruce Coleman/John Canalosi. **p13** (top) Robert Pickett/CORBIS, (bottom) Julie Habel/CORBIS. **p15** Stockbyte. **p17** GettyImages/JH Pete Carmichael. **p19** Martin B. Withers/CORBIS. **p20** © Malie Rich-Griffith/infocusphotos.com. **p21** Christian Decout/Still Pictures. **p23** Roland Seitre/Still Pictures. **p24** Philip Perry/CORBIS. **p25** Bruno Pambour/Still Pictures. **p26** Xavier Eichaker/Still Pictures. **p27** FLPA - Images of Nature © Minden Pictures. **p29** © Natural History Museum, London. **p31** Stockbyte.

First published in 2002 by Usborne Publishing Ltd., Usborne House, 83-85 Saffron Hill, London EC1N 8RT, England. www.usborne.com  Copyright © 2002 Usborne Publishing Ltd. The name Usborne and the devices ♀ ⊕ are Trade Marks of Usborne Publishing Ltd. All rights reserved. No part of this publication may be reproduced, stored in a retrieval system, or transmitted in any form or by any means, electronic, mechanical, photocopying, recording or otherwise without the prior permission of the publisher.
First published in America 2003. U.E. Printed in Belgium.

# Internet safety rules

- Ask your parent's or guardian's permission before you connect to the Internet.

- When you are on the Internet, never tell anyone your full name, address or telephone number, and ask an adult before you give your e-mail address.

- If a Web site asks you to log in or register by typing your name or e-mail address, ask an adult's permission first.

- If you do receive an e-mail from someone you don't know, tell an adult and do not reply to the e-mail.

## Notes for parents or guardians

The Web sites described in this book are regularly reviewed and the links in Usborne Quicklinks are updated. However, the content of a Web site may change at any time and Usborne Publishing is not responsible, and does not accept liability, for the content or availability of any Web site other than its own, or for any exposure to harmful, offensive or inaccurate material which may appear on the Web. We recommend that children are supervised while on the Internet, that they do not use Internet Chat Rooms and that you use Internet filtering software to block unsuitable material. Please ensure that your children follow the safety guidelines printed above. For more information, see the "Net Help" area on the Usborne Quicklinks Web site at **www.usborne-quicklinks.com**